Making Muffins

Learning the Fractions $\frac{1}{2}$, $\frac{1}{3}$, and $\frac{1}{4}$

Susan Vaughan

Math
for the
REAL World™

Rosen Classroom Books & Materials
New York

Sara and Tom want to make some **muffins**.
Sara's mom will help them.

Sara's mom turns on the oven. Sara finds a
pan that holds 12 muffins.

Tom reads the **directions** on the box.

Sara puts the muffin mix in a bowl.

1 cup

$\frac{1}{2}$ cup

Sara **stirs** 1 cup of milk into the mix.

Then she adds another $\frac{1}{2}$ cup of milk.

Sara adds an egg to the mix.

Sara adds $\frac{1}{4}$ cup of oil. Tom stirs everything together with a big spoon.

Tom stirs $\frac{1}{3}$ cup of berries into the **batter**.

Sara puts muffin cups into the pan. Sara and
Tom pour the batter into the cups.

Sara's mom puts the muffins in the oven.

The muffins take about 25 minutes to **bake**.

After the muffins are done, Sara and Tom let
them cool. Then the muffins are ready to eat!

Glossary

bake (BAKE) To cook something in the oven.

batter (BA-tuhr) A mix made mostly of flour, oil, water, and eggs.

directions (duh-REK-shunz) A list that tells you how to do something.

muffin (MUH-fun) A kind of small, round cake.

stir (STUHR) To use a spoon to mix things together in a bowl.